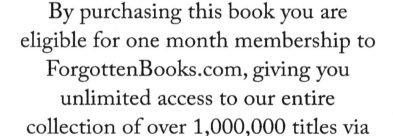

ISBN 978-0-260-86142-9
PIBN 10543838

Forgotten Books is a registered trademark of FB &c Ltd.
Copyright © 2018 FB &c Ltd.
FB &c Ltd, Dalton House, 60 Windsor Avenue, London, SW19 2RR.
Company number 08720141. Registered in England and Wales.

For support please visit www.forgottenbooks.com

United States
Department of
Agriculture

National
Agricultural
Library

Beltsville
Maryland
20705

The Status and Potential of Aquaculture in the United States: An Overview and Bibliography

July 1993

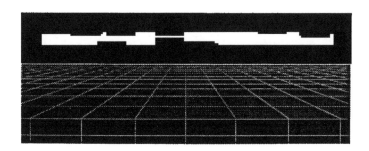

The Status and Potential of Aquaculture in the United States: An Overview and Bibliography

Background

Aquaculture is the fastest growing segment of agriculture in the United States. Although the farming of aquatic plants and animals was practiced prior to 2000 BC in China, it was not until the early 1870's that aquaculture began taking roots in the United States. Trout farming is considered the oldest farming industry in the United States and began as a way to replenish wild stock in streams and lakes. In the 1930's, President Franklin D. Rosevelt established a "Farm Pond" program. This program provided government assistance to farmers in the construction and stocking of ponds with fish to increase their income.

Over the past twelve years, aquaculture has shown considerable growth. In 1980, aquaculture production was 203 million pounds with a farm gate value of $192 million. By 1990, these numbers more than quadrupled with production reaching 860 million pounds with a farm gate value of over $760 million (a four-fold increase since 1980). In 1991, U.S. aquaculture had a farm gate value of $880 million. This accounts for an economic impact of over $8 million annually and the creation of nearly 300,000 aquaculture-related jobs. Yet, despite this significant growth, domestic aquaculture only supplies 10-15 percent of U.S. seafood needs.

Much of the aquaculture expansion is driven by an increased demand for fisheries products and reduced yields from traditional fisheries landings. During the 1980's, U.S. imports of fisheries products more than doubled to $9.6 billion, resulting in a substantial trade deficit of $4.9 billion in 1989. After Japan, the United States is the second largest importer of seafood products. In 1990, more than $9 billion worth of imported fish and shellfish were imported, $800 million of which was farm-raised.

The U.S. Congress declared the following in the National Aquaculture Act of 1980:

> "...aquaculture has the potential for reducing the United States trade deficit in fisheries products, for augmenting existing commercial and recreational fisheries, and for producing other renewable resources, thereby assisting the United States in meeting its future food needs and contributing to the solution of world resource problems."

Today, interest in aquaculture continues to grow. U.S. fish farms cultivate approximately 30 different species of fish and shellfish. There has also been an increase in aquatic plant culture in the United States which has value in the food, drug, and cosmetic industries. American aquaculture will help satisfy seafood demand, provide an alternative agricultural opportunity, provide jobs for displaced commercial fishermen and the rural community, and reduce the trade deficit.

Seafood Consumption

Over the years, consumers have shown an increased demand for fish and shellfish in the

United States. The U.S. per capita consumption of seafood has risen from 12.5 pounds of edible meat in 1980 to 15 pounds of edible meat in 1993, a 20 percent increase. This is due, in part, to the growing interest by Americans in the health and dietary benefits of seafood.

The aquaculture industry strives to provide Americans with high quality, fresh, dependable, and nutritious seafood products. The majority of 1991 sales were for fresh and frozen seafoods vs. canned and cured (salted, pickled, dried) fishery products. One example is fresh or frozen shrimp which rose from 0.2 pound per person in 1990 to 2.4 pounds per person in 1991. Much of this growth was supplied by farm-raised shrimp.

The Department of Commerce has projected that U.S. consumption of seafood could increase by 30 percent by the year 2000, requiring an additional demand of one billion pounds annually. If this expansion occurs, greater domestic aquaculture production will be required to help satisfy consumers' demand for seafood.

In coordination with industry, the Federal government places strong emphasis on quality assurance of aquaculture products. The Joint Subcommittee on Aquaculture, a Federal Government-wide coordinating body of 23 representatives of 12 Departments or agencies, established a Working Group on Quality Assurance in Aquaculture Production in 1990. This group consists of government and industry representatives and addresses quality assurance issues in aquaculture, including the use of drugs and chemicals in aquaculture production. These efforts will continue to ensure quality of U.S. aquaculture products for the consumer.

Farmed Species

Overview

Aquaculture species grown in the United States include finfish (catfish, trout, salmon, striped bass, tilapia, baitfish, ornamental fish, and other species), crustaceans (crawfish, shrimp, and others), mollusks (oysters, clams, mussels, and others), and aquatic plants (including seaweed). Producers in the United States range from corporations employing several hundred workers to small family farms.

About 12 to 14 percent of the seafood we consume today is farm-raised. According to USDA, this figure should double within 10 years. About one-half of the U.S. aquaculture is **catfish**, but over 30 species are cultured in the nation today. **Crawfish** is the second largest domestically produced aquaculture species on a quantity basis. On a value basis, crawfish ranks third, behind catfish and trout. Marine aquaculture makes up approximately 20 percent of U.S. aquaculture.

Marine aquaculture in the United States is dominated by salmon and oyster culture, which represents about 80 percent of the total. Other species that make up the remaining 20 percent are clams, mussels, and shrimp. Abalone, red drum, scallops, and striped bass are also being commercially produced to a lesser degree.

Catfish. Catfish farming originated in the southeastern United States in the late 1950's. It is the largest aquaculture industry in the United States. Today, about half of total U.S aquaculture production comes from the catfish industry. Advances in production technologies in the areas of genetic improvements, feeds, aeration, and new strategies to control diseases and off-flavor will continue to help boost the growth of this industry. Between 1975-1991, catfish production increased more than 2,400 percent, transforming the catfish industry into a major force in the domestic seafood market. Since 1991, production has continued to grow, with an expansion in 1992 of almost 20 percent. Mississippi is the focal point of the U.S. catfish industry and accounted for over 70 percent of total sales.

In 1992, catfish sales to processing plants totaled 457.4 million pounds, a jump of 17 percent from the previous year. In the first quarter alone, over 120 million pounds were processed, more than was processed in all of 1982. The large increase in sales can be attributed chiefly to low farm-level from the end of 1991 through the first half of 1992, as growers worked off excess inventories. Much of the decline in the farm-level price was passed through in the form of lower wholesale prices, which in turn spurred higher sales.

Farm-level catfish prices fell five percent to average just under 60 cents a pound for 1992-- the lowest annual average since 1982. However, prices began to strengthen in the second half of the year. Farm prices should continue to move upward during 1993 in response to lower available supplies.

As of January 1, 1993, results of a National Agricultural Statistics Service (NASS) grower survey reported that there were 1,527 catfish growers in the United States. The area used in catfish ponds was 151,860 acres. The states of Mississippi, Alabama, Arkansas, and Louisiana account for over 90 percent of this acreage.

Crawfish. Crawfish are found naturally throughout the continental United States, but are currently commercially grown in only a few states. The red swamp crawfish, *Procambarus clarkii*, and the white river crawfish, *Procambarus acutus acutus*, are two species of commercial importance in the United States. The red swamp crawfish is the primary species cultured because it produces more consistent yields and is more valued in international and southern United States markets. In the southern United States, there are more than 140,000 acres of crawfish ponds. Most of the acreage is in southern Louisiana with a small production area in southeastern Texas. Production averages 500 pounds per acre but can reach around 4,000 pounds per acre. From 1988 to 1990, crawfish production rose from 62.9 million pounds to 70.7 million. Growers' sales in 1990 were valued at $34 million. During 1992, the crawfish industry exported 7.3 million pounds, 13 percent more than in 1991. The exports were valued at $14.8 million.

Hybrid Striped Bass. Although the government does not provide production statistics for hybrid striped bass (HSB), the Striped Bass Growers' Association (SBGA) estimated U.S. production to be 1.4 million pounds (live-weight) in 1990 and 3.4-3.7 million pounds in 1991. Production estimates for 1992 are higher at approximately five million pounds. The most commonly cultured HSB is a cross between a female striped bass (*Morone saxatilis*) and a male white bass (*Morone chrysops*).

As production continues to grow, there is a concomitant need to develop new markets throughout the United States beyond the traditional northeastern whole fish markets to avoid a decline in food market prices. There is no direct competition from production in foreign countries, which currently have no ready markets. The small size of the wild catch of striped bass has helped support the continued growth of the hybrid striped bass industry.

3

Mollusks. Washington State is probably the nation's largest producer of farmed-raised mollusks. In 1990, oyster production (*Crassostrea gigas*) was about eight million pounds and valued at $17.3 million. Also in 1990, Washington growers reported production of 3.4 million pounds of Manila clams (*Tapes philippinarum*) valued at $5 million. Washington farmers also produced almost 590,000 pounds of mussels (*Mytilus edulis*) valued at $800,000. Other States also have farm-raised mollusk industries although the reporting of production is spotty. On the East and Gulf coasts, oyster production is chiefly the American oyster (*Crassostrea virginica*). Florida growers reported sales of $1.4 million in 1991, while Maryland growers reported sales of 12,430 bushels. In various areas along the East coast, there are hard clam farms. Florida clam farmers reported sales of $1.2 million in 1991.

Salmon. The domestic farm-raised salmon industry faces strong competition from domestic wild catch as well as foreign wild catch and farm-raised product. Farm-raised salmon primarily consists of Atlantic, coho, and chinook. Atlantic salmon is becoming the predominant species raised in the United States because, in a culture situation, it has some advantages over other species.

In 1992, production of U.S. farm-raised salmon was estimated at 19 million pounds (live-weight). This represents a large increase from 1991, as production in Maine rose to 13 million pounds in 1992, up considerably from the previous year.

The U.S. farm-raised salmon industry is greatly influenced by foreign competition. In 1992, fresh farm-raised Atlantic salmon imports totaled $127 million, up 17 percent from a year earlier. Canada and Chile were the dominant suppliers, each country accounting for over 90 percent of imports.

Shrimp. During the 1980's, foreign production of farm-raised shrimp increased dramatically, making aquaculture a major force in the shrimp industry. In 1991, world production of marine shrimp was approximately 1.5 billion pounds. The largest expansion has been in China, Thailand, Ecuador, and Indonesia.

In the United States, there is a great deal of enthusiasm in shrimp culture due to the commercial success in other countries. In 1992, U.S. production of farm-raised marine shrimp was about 4.4 million pounds (live-weight). Growers in Hawaii, Texas, and South Carolina have developed viable production systems.

Production of disease-free broodstock and post larvae may be an important new market for the U.S. shrimp industry. Many major producing countries have had problems with disease outbreaks. The use of certified disease-free shrimp could increase production efficiency through improved feed conversion rates and lowered mortality.

Tilapia. Production of tilapia in the United States has continued to grow, reaching approximately nine million pounds (live-weight) in 1992, according to the American Tilapia Growers Association. Its history as a food fish dates back to around 2,000 BC. Tilapia has been grown commercially in Africa and Asia for local consumption. In 1991, more than nine million pounds of tilapia were imported into the United States through southern California.

Since tilapia culture requires warm water, outdoor production in the United States is

4

limited to those states that are climatically suitable. In other areas, tilapia production takes place indoors through tank systems. By expanding the use of indoor systems, tilapia production could expand in areas closer to major markets. An advantage to U.S. growers would be the provision of fresh and live tilapia in contrast to frozen imports.

Trout. The 1992 USDA annual survey of 461 trout operations over a one-year period (September 1, 1991-August 31, 1992) showed sales at $67.0 million, down 4 percent from 1991. Idaho is the largest producer, with sales in 1992 at $28.5 million. Production in this State is expected to continue at a steady pace with fairly stable prices for food-size fish.

Pennsylvania's growers had the second highest sales with $6.4 million, up 54 percent from the previous year. Sales in Washington, North Carolina, and California all totaled between $5.3 and $5.9. Future expansion of the trout industry outside of Idaho is dependent upon the availability of adequate water supplies.

Outlook for the United States

The importance of aquaculture has increased dramatically in the United States. This can be seen by the four-fold increase in aquaculture production from 1980-1990, the creation of nearly 300,000 jobs in 1991, and the 20 percent increase in per capita consumption of fish and shellfish in the 1980's to 15 pounds today. Domestic aquaculture provides opportunity for alternative agriculture, helps reduce the trade deficit, and helps satisfy the continued demand for seafood. The U.S. Department of Commerce estimated that by the year 2000, an additional one billion pounds of seafood would be required to satisfy demand. The trend for production of edible and nonedible products is growing fast and expected to continue in the future. Changing consumer preferences for seafood products and the prices of farm-raised products relative to wild-caught products may be major factors in the future growth of aquaculture.

There is significant potential for marine aquaculture in the United States. In 1990, culture of marine species accounted for approximately 20 percent of the U.S. aquaculture production and value. The Departments of Agriculture, Commerce, and Interior, and the National Science Foundation continue to annually support research and development, education, information, and conservation programs in marine aquaculture. According to the Federal Coordinating Council on Science, Engineering, and Technology (February 1992), there is a significant U.S. market for extracts derived from marine algae, such agar, algenic acid, or carrageenan.

Growth of the domestic aquaculture industry in the 1990's will be affected by a variety of issues including: 1) public perception of seafood safety; 2) changing industry structure for production and marketing; 3) emergence of new aquaculture species in the United States and abroad; and 4) increasing competition from foreign producers and domestic competitors.

With continued emphasis on quality assurance, good marketing practices, education and information programs, aquaculture management, land availability, high-quality water, new production technologies, and genetic improvement, the future of aquaculture in the U.S. looks bright!

5

6

BIBLIOGRAPHY

[Anonymous] "Aquaculture: An industry with a future for
    Appalachia." *Appalachia*, Winter 1990, v. 23 (1), pp. 17-21.
    NAL Call No.: HC107.A13A6

Barnett, Jane. *A Review of the U.S. Farm-Raised Catfish Industry
    and its Implications for Canadian Groundfish Exporters.*
    Economic and Commercial Analysis Directorate, Department of
    Fisheries and Oceans, Market Analysis Group, Ottawa, Canada.
    July 1990. 46 pp.
    NAL Call No.: HD9469.C382C222 1990

Beem, Marley. "Aquaculture: Realities and potentials when
    getting started." Southern Regional Aquaculture Center,
    SRAC Publication No. 441, 1991, 8 pp.
    NAL Call No.: SH151.S62

de la Bretonne, Larry W., Jr. and Robert P. Romaire. "Crawfish
    production: Harvesting, marketing and economics." Southern
    Regional Aquaculture Center, *SRAC Publication* No. 242, Jan.
    1990, 4 pp.
    NAL Call No.: SH151.S62

Broussard, M.C., Jr. "Aquaculture: Opportunities for the
    nineties." *Journal of Animal Science*, Oct. 1991, v. 69
    (10), pp. 4221-4228.
    NAL Call No.: 49 J82

Burrage, David. "The Mississippi shrimp industry, a management
    perspective." Proceedings of a Mississippi Sea Grant
    Advisory Service Workshop, April 12, 1989. Sponsored by the
    NOAA/National Sea Grant College Program, U.S. Department of
    Commerce. 1989, Publication no. MASGP-89-029, 50 pp.
    NAL Call No.: SH380.62.U5M5

Buttner, Joe. "Aquaculture species for the Northeast." *NRAC
    Fact Sheet* No. 130, Northeastern Regional Aquaculture Center
    (University of Massachusetts - Dartmouth, North Dartmouth,
    MA 02747), 1992, 4 pp.

Buttner, Joe. "Aquaculture systems for the Northeast." *NRAC
    Fact Sheet* No. 120, Northeastern Regional Aquaculture Center
    (University of Massachusetts - Dartmouth, North Dartmouth,
    MA 02747), 1992, 4 pp.

Buttner, Joe. "Is aquatic farming for you?" *NRAC Fact Sheet* No.
    101, Northeastern Regional Aquaculture Center (University of
    Massachusetts - Dartmouth, North Dartmouth, MA 02747), 1991,
    2 pp.

Capps, Oral, Jr. and Johannes Adrianus Lambregts. "Analysis of a
     local retail market for catfish and crawfish." Southern
     Regional Aquaculture Center, SRAC Publication No. 512, Nov.
     1990, 36 pp.
     NAL Call No.: SH151.S62

Chamberlain, George W. "Texas aquaculture: Status of the
     Industry. Review draft for 1990 Texas Aquaculture
     Conference, Jan. 30-Feb. 1, 1990, Corpus Christi, Texas.
     Sponsored by Texas Aquaculture Association, Texas
     Agricultural Extension Service, Texas A & M University Sea
     Grant College Program. 1990, 133 pp.
     NAL Call No.: SH135.T49 1990

Chew, Kenneth K. and Derrick Toba. Western Regional Aquaculture
     Industry Situation and Outlook Report. Volume 2 (1986
     through 1991). Western Regional Aquaculture Center,
     University of Washington, College of Ocean & Fisheries
     Sciences, School of Fisheries. March 1993. 24 pp. +
     Appendices.
     NAL Call No.: HD9457.A17C43

Decker, E.A., A.D. Crum, S.D. Mims, and J.H. Tidwell.
     "Processing yield and composition of paddlefish (Polyodon
     spathula), a potential aquaculture species." Journal of
     Agricultural and Food Chemistry, Apr. 1991, v. 39 (4), pp.
     686-688.
     NAL Call No.: 381 J8223

Dicks, M.R. and D.J. Harvey. "Outlook for U.S. aquaculture."
     Outlook - Proceedings, Agricultural Outlook Conference, U.S.
     Department of Agriculture, Washington, DC, April 1990,
     pp. 163-172.
     NAL Call No.: 1.90 C2OU8

Dunham, R.A. "Outlook for genetics research and application in
     aquaculture." Paper presented at "New opportunities for
     agriculture," December 3-5, 1991, Washington, DC. Outlook -
     Proceedings, Agricultural Outlook Conference, U.S.
     Department of Agriculture, Washington, DC, 1992 (68th), pp.
     137-148.
     NAL Call No.: 1.90 C2OU8

Engle, Carole R., Larry W. Dorman, and D. Leroy Gray. "Baitfish
     production: Enterprise budget." Southern Regional
     Aquaculture Center, SRAC Publication No. 122, Nov. 1988,
     4 pp.
     NAL Call No.: SH151.S62

Engle, C.R. and N.M. Stone. "Preparing a business proposal for aquaculture loans." University of Arkansas, Cooperative Extension Service, Little Rock, Arkansas. Nov. 1991 (334), 10 pp.
NAL Call No.: 275.29 AR4MI

Evans, M. "Aquaculture laying groundwork for future growth." *Farmline*, Washington, DC, May 1992, v. 13 (5), pp. 12-14.
NAL Call No.: aHD1401.A2U52

Food and Agriculture Organization of the United Nations. Fishery Information, Data, and Statistics Service, Rome, Italy. "Aquaculture production (1984-1990)." *FAO Fisheries Circular* no. 815, Rev. 4, June 1992, 206 pp.
[English, French, and Spanish]
NAL Call No.: SH1.F59 no.815

Frobish, Lowell T. "Retail grocery markets for catfish." Alabama Agricultural Experiment Station, Auburn University, AL, Bulletin 611, July 1991, 44 pp.

Garling, D.L. "Making plans for commercial aquaculture in the North Central Region." *NCRAC Fact Sheet Series* #101 (North Central Regional Aquaculture Center, Dept. Animal Ecology, 124 Science II, Iowa State University, Ames, IA 50011), March 1992, 5 pp.

Geiger, Russell A. *Costs and Configurations of Alternative Tilapia Production Systems.* Thesis (M.S.), University of Florida. 1990. 139 leaves.
FU Call No.: LD1780 1990.C312

Gilbert, R.J. "Small-scale marketing of aquaculture products." Southern Regional Aquaculture Center, *SRAC Publication* No. 350 (Southern Regional Aquaculture Center, Delta Branch Experiment Station, P.O. Box 197, Stoneville, MS 38776), August 1989, 4 pp.
NAL Call No.: SH151.S62

Hanson, J.S. *Developing an Aquaculture Business Proposal.* Texas A & M University, Department of Agricultural Economics, College Station, Texas. 1991. (various pagings)
NAL Call No.: HD1401.F32 no.FP91-1

Hargreaves, John A. and Dallas E. Alston. "Status and potential of aquaculture in the Caribbean." Proceedings of a workshop sponsored by the Gulf and Caribbean Fisheries Association, 10-11 November 1988, St. Thomas, US Virgin Islands. In: *Advances in World Aquaculture*, v. 5, World Aquaculture Society, Baton Rouge, LA. 1991. 274 pp.
NAL Call No.: SH42.S73 1991

9

Harvey, D.J. "Aquaculture: A diverse industry poised for growth." *Food Review*, Oct./Dec. 1991, v. 14 (4), pp. 18-23.
NAL Call No.: aHD9001.N275
Abstract: Aquaculture has become a prominent industry in the U.S. But a variety of resource constraints, environmental issues, and food safety concerns will make continued expansion more of a challenge. This article discusses these issues.

Harvey, D.J. "Aquaculture production rising." *Agricultural Outlook*, U.S. Department of Agriculture, Economic Research Service, Washington, DC, Nov. 1991 (180), pp. 14-16.
NAL Call No.: aHD1751.A42

Harvey, D.J. "Outlook for U.S. aquaculture." Paper presented at "Agriculture in a world of change," Nov. 27-29, 1990, Washington, DC. Outlook - Proceedings, Agricultural Outlook Conference, U.S. Department of Agriculture, Washington, DC, March 1991 (67th), pp. 188-198.
NAL Call No.: 1.90 C2OU8

Harvey, David. Commodity Economics Division, Economic Research Service, U.S. Department of Agriculture, Washington, DC. *Aquaculture Situation and Outlook Report* AQUA-10, March 1993, 46 pp. [Issued Biannually]
NAL Call No.: aHD9454.A92

Harvey, P. *Hybrid Striped Bass Aquaculture Survey and the Market Potential.* Department of Marine Advisory Services, Virginia Institute of Marine Science, College of William and Mary, Virginia. 1990. 77 pp.
NAL Call No.: HD 9457.V8H9

Hinshaw, J.M. "Trout farming: A guide to production and inventory management." Southern Regional Aquaculture Center, *SRAC Publication* No. 222, Jan. 1990, 2 pp.
NAL Call No.: SH151.S62

Hinshaw, Jeffrey and Mike Gray. "Trout production in the Southeast." Videocassette (19 min., 48 sec.); 3/4 in. Produced by Department of Agricultural Communications, North Carolina State University. Funded by Southern Regional Aquaculture Center. 1990.
NAL Call No.: Videocassette no.957

Hinshaw, Jeffrey and Mike Gray. "Trout production in the Southeast." Videocassette (19 min., 48 sec.); 1/2 in. Produced by Department of Agricultural Communications, North Carolina State University. Funded by Southern Regional Aquaculture Center. 1990.
NAL Call No.: Videocassette no.931

Hinshaw, J.M., L.E. Rogers, and J.E. Easley. "Budgets for trout production: Estimated costs and returns for trout farming in the South." *SRAC Publication* No. 221, Southern Regional Aquaculture Center, Jan. 1990, 7 pp. NAL Call No.: SH151.S62

Hodson, Ronald G. and Maureen Hayes. "Hybrid striped bass: Pond production of foodfish." Southern Regional Aquaculture Center, *SRAC Publication* No. 303, July 1989, 2 pp. NAL Call No.: SH151.S62

Johnsen, P.B. "Aquaculture product quality issues: Market position opportunities under mandatory seafood inspection regulations." *Journal of Animal Science*, Oct. 1991, v. 69 (10), pp. 4209-4215. NAL Call No.: 49 J82

Joint Subcommittee on Aquaculture. *Aquaculture in the United States: Status, Opportunities, and Recommendations. A Report to the Federal Coordinating Council on Science, Engineering, and Technology.* Joint Subcommittee on Aquaculture coordinating administrative office: Cooperative State Research Service, U.S. Department of Agriculture, Aerospace Building, Suite 342, 14th & Independence Ave., SW, Washington, DC 20250-2200. May 1992. 20 pp.

Kruppenbach, Rebecca C. and James T. Davis. "Computer software for aquaculture: Descriptions and evaluations." Southern Regional Aquaculture Center, *SRAC Publication* No. 380, July 1989, 8 pp. NAL Call No.: SH151.S62

Ladewig, Katheleen F. and Donna W. Logan. "You can do catfish." Southern Regional Aquaculture Center, *SRAC Publication* No. 501, Nov. 1992, 4 pp. NAL Call No.: SH151.S62

Lichtkoppler, Frank R. "Factors to consider in establishing a successful aquaculture business in the North Central Region." *North Central Regional Aquaculture Center. Technical Bulletin Series* #106, Michigan State University, 13 Natural Resources Building, East Lansing, MI 48824-1222, January 1993, 8 pp.

Lichtkoppler, Frank R. and James M. Ebeling. "Is aquaculture for you?" Ohio Sea Grant College Program, Ohio State University, 1314 Kinnear Road, Columbus, OH 43212-1194. OHSU-FS-039, Revised 1991, 2 pp.

Losordo, T.M., J.E. Easley, and P.W. Westerman. "The preliminary
    results of a feasibility study of fish production in
    recirculating aquaculture systems." Paper presented at the
    "1989 International Winter Meeting sponsored by the American
    Society of Agricultural Engineers," December 12-15, 1989,
    New Orleans, Louisiana. Paper - American Society of
    Agricultural Engineers, Winter 1989 (89-7557), 17 pp.
    NAL Call No.: 290.9 AM32P

Losordo, Thomas M., Michael Masser, and James Rakocy.
    "Recirculating aquaculture tank production systems: An
    overview of critical considerations." Southern Regional
    Aquaculture Center, *SRAC Publication* No. 451, Jan. 1992,
    6 pp.
    NAL Call No.: SH151.S62

McGowan, Sandra. *The Fish and Shellfish Industry: Aquaculture
    and the U.S. Seafood Market.* "Market research studies to
    prepare today's business executive for tomorrow's events"--
    cover, Business Communications Co. October 1989.
    152 leaves.
    NAL Call No.: HD9455.F57

McGowan, Sandra. *Opportunities in Aquaculture.* Companion to
    BCC's previously published "The fish and shellfish
    industry", Business Communications Co. July 1990.
    200 leaves.
    NAL Call No.: HD9455.O6

McVey, Eileen M. *Aquaculture for Youth and Youth Educators.*
    Available from Aquaculture Information Center, National
    Agricultural Library, Room 304, 10301 Baltimore Blvd.,
    Beltsville, MD 20705-2351. Revised April 1993. 35 pp.

McVey, Eileen M. *Current Research in Shrimp Culture.*
    Bibliography available from Aquaculture Information Center,
    National Agricultural Library, Room 304, 10301 Baltimore
    Blvd., Beltsville, MD 20705-2351. April 1992. 14 pp.

National Marine Fisheries Service, Fisheries Statistics Division,
    National Oceanic and Atmospheric Administration, U.S.
    Department of Commerce. "Fisheries of the United States,
    1991." *Current Fishery Statistics* No. 9100, May 1992,
    113 pp.
    NAL Call No.: 156.2 St23 No.9100

National Research Council, Committee on Assessment of Technology and Opportunities for Marine Aquaculture in the United States, Marine Board. *Marine Aquaculture Opportunities for Growth: Report of the Committee on Assessment of Technology and Opportunities for Marine Aquaculture in the United States.* National Academy Press, Washington, DC. 1992. 290 pp.

Nerrie, B.L. "Aquaculture, fishing and other income opportunities from aquatic systems." In: *Conference Proceedings: Income Opportunities for the Private Landowner Through Management of Natural Resources and Recreational Access* (April 9-12, 1989, Wheeling, W.Va). Edited by William N. Grafton [et al.], 1990, pp. 137-146.
NAL Call No.: GV191.6.I52 1989

Pomeroy, R.S., J.C.O. Nyankori, and D.C. Israel. "Aquaculture products in the market place: Utilization of catfish products by full-service restaurants in the United States." *Journal of International Food & Agribusiness Marketing*, 1991, v. 3 (1), pp. 1-17.
NAL Call No.: YHD9000.1.J6

Pomeroy, Robert S., James C.O. Nyankori, and Danilo C. Israel. "Aquaculture products in the market place: Utilization of fish and seafood and catfish products by full-service restaurants in the United States." Southern Regional Aquaculture Center, *SRAC Publication* No. 510, June 1990, 80 pp.
NAL Call No.: SH151.S62
[same authors & title produced by Clemson Univ., Dept. Agric. Economics and Rural Sociol., South Carolina Agric. Exper. Station, SC, June 1990 (464), 91 pp., NAL Call No.: 281.9 C59]

Pomeroy, R.S., J.C.O. Nyankori, and D.C. Israel. "Aquaculture products in the market place: Utilization of catfish products by full-service restaurants in the United States." Clemson University, Department of Agricultural Economics and Rural Sociology, South Carolina Agricultural Experiment Station, Clemson, S.C., SRAC Publication 510, June 1990, 80 pp.
NAL Call No.: 281.9 C59

Pounds, Larry W. Dorman and Carole R. Engle. "An economic analysis of baitfish production in Arkansas." Report series (University of Arkansas, Fayetteville, Agricultural Experiment Station), 321, Dec. 1991, 29 pp.
NAL Call No.: 100 AR42R no.321

Rakocy, James E. and Andrew S. McGinty. "Pond culture of
    tilapia." Southern Regional Aquaculture Center, *SRAC
    Publication* No. 280, July 1989, 4 pp.
    NAL Call No.: SH151.S62

Regenstein, Joe M. "Processing and marketing aquacultured fish."
    NRAC Fact Sheet No. 140, Northeastern Regional Aquaculture
    Center (University of Massachusetts - Dartmouth, North
    Dartmouth, MA 02747), 1992, 4 pp.

Roberts, K.J.; D.G. Marschall; and J. Homziak. "Economic
    potential of aquaculture in dredged material containment
    areas." Cooperative Extension Service, Mississippi State
    University, Apr. 1992 (1823), 19 pp.
    NAL Call No.: 275.29 M68EXT

Snyder, F.L. "Aquaculture opportunities." *Journal of Extension*,
    Madison, Wisconsin, Fall 1992, v. 30, pp. 23-25.
    NAL Call No.: 275.28 J82

Swann, LaDon. *Basic Overview of Aquaculture*. Aquaculture
    Extension Illinois-Indiana Sea Grant Program, Purdue
    University Cooperative Extension Service, West Lafayette,
    Indiana. 1990. 11 pp.
    NAL Call No.: SH34.S92 1990

Swann, L. *A Basic Overview of Aquaculture*. Cooperative
    Extension Service, Purdue University, West Lafayette,
    Indiana. July 1990 (457). 12 pp.
    NAL Call No.: 49.9 IN23

Swann, LaDon. "A basic overview of aquaculture: History, water
    quality, types of aquaculture, production methods." *North
    Central Regional Aquaculture Center. Technical Bulletin
    Series* #102, Michigan State University, 13 Natural Resources
    Building, East Lansing, MI 48824-1222, August 1992, 10 pp.

Technology Management Group. *Biological Products for
    Aquaculture: A Worldwide Market Study on Vaccines,
    Therapeutics, Diagnostics, Hormones and Genetic
    Manipulations*. 1 v. (various pagings). New Haven, CT:
    Technology Management Group. Jan. 1990. "Confidential
    information; do not copy"--at foot of every page.
    NAL Call No.: HD9450.5.B5

Thunberg, E.M., C.M. Adams, and C.E. Cichra. "Economic,
    regulatory, and technological barriers to entry into the
    Florida aquaculture industry." Economic information
    report - University of Florida, Food and Resource Economics
    Department, Agricultural Experiment Station, Gainesville,
    Florida. Dec. 1991 (91-8), 42 pp.
    NAL Call No.: HD9007.F6F6

Thunberg, E.M., C.M. Adams, and C.E. Cichra. "Economic,
regulatory, and technological barriers to entry into the
Florida aquaculture industry." Paper prepared for
presentation at the Florida Aquaculture Association
Meetings, Miami, Florida, October 22-24, 1991. Staff paper
(University of Florida, Food and Resource Economics Dept.,
Inst. Food and Agric. Sci., Gainesville). Oct. 1991, 27 pp.
NAL Call No.: HD1751.A1S73 no.SP91-34

Tiddens, Art. "Aquaculture in America: The Role of Science,
Government, and the Entrepreneur." Westview Press, Boulder,
Colorado. 1990. 191 pp.
NAL Call No.: HD9455.T53

University of Arkansas (System), Cooperative Extension Service.
Arkansas Aquaculture Plan Current Status and Potential.
University of Arkansas Cooperative Extension Service
Program, Pine Bluff, Arkansas. 1991. 80 pp.
NAL Call No.: HD947.A8A75 1991

Warren, H. "Catfish industry perspective." Paper presented at
"Agriculture in a world of change," Nov. 27-29, 1990,
Washington, DC. Outlook - Proceedings, Agricultural Outlook
Conference, U.S. Department of Agriculture, Washington, DC,
March 1991 (67th), pp. 199-205.
NAL Call No.: 1.90 C2OU8

Webster, Don, Donald Meritt, and George J. Flick. *Aquaculture in
Maryland & Virginia: Problems, Politics and Potential.* A
summary from a conference held June 8 and 9, 1988 in
Waldorf, Maryland. Maryland Sea Grant College. 1989.
31 pp.
NAL Call No.: SH35.A12A68 1988

United States Department of Agriculture	National Agricultural Library	Public Services Division	Beltsville, Maryland 20705

Document Delivery Services to Individuals

The National Agricultural Library (NAL) supplies agricultural materials not found elsewhere to other libraries.

Filling requests for materials readily available from other sources diverts NAL's resources and diminishes its ability to serve as a national source for agricultural and agriculturally related materials. Therefore, NAL is viewed as a library of last resort. Submit requests first to local or state library sources prior to sending to NAL. In the United States, possible sources are public libraries, land-grant university or other large research libraries within a state. In other countries submit requests through major university, national, or provincial institutions.

If the needed publications are not available from these sources, submit requests to NAL with a statement indicating their non-availability. Submit one request per page following the instructions for libraries below.

NAL's Document Delivery Service Information for the Library

The following information is provided to assist your librarian in obtaining the required materials.

Loan Service — Materials in NAL's collection are loaned only to other U.S. libraries. Requests for loans are made through local public, academic, or special libraries.

The following materials are not available for loan: serials (except USDA serials); rare, reference, and reserve books; microforms; and proceedings of conferences or symposia. Photocopy or microform of non-circulating publications may be purchased as described below.

Document Delivery Service — Photocopies of articles are available for a fee. Make requests through local public, academic, or special libraries. The library will submit a separate interlibrary loan form for each article or item requested. If the citation is from an NAL database (CAIN/AGRICOLA, *Bibliography of Agriculture,* or the NAL Catalog) and the call number is given, put that call number in the proper block on the request form. Willingness to pay charges must be indicated on the form. Include compliance with copyright law or a statement that the article is for "research purposes only" on the interlibrary loan form or letter. Requests cannot be processed without these statements.

Charges

- Photocopy, hard copy of microfilm and microfiche – $5.00 for the first 10 pages or fraction copied from a single article or publication. $3.00 for each additional 10 pages or fraction.
- Duplication of NAL-owned microfilm – $10.00 per reel.
- Duplication of NAL-owned microfiche – $5.00 for the first fiche and $.50 for each additional fiche per title.

Billing – Charges include postage and handling, and are subject to change. Invoices are issued quarterly by the National Technical Information Service (NTIS), 5285 Port Royal Road, Springfield, VA 22161. Establishing a deposit account with NTIS is encouraged. *DO NOT SEND PREPAYMENT.*

Send Requests to:

> USDA, National Agricultural Library
> Document Delivery Services Branch, PhotoLab
> 10301 Baltimore Blvd , NAL Bldg.
> Beltsville, Maryland 20705-2351

Contact the Head, Document Delivery Services Branch in writing or by calling (301) 504-5755 with questions or comments about this policy.

 National Agricultural Library

ELECTRONIC MAIL ACCESS FOR INTERLIBRARY LOAN (ILL) REQUESTS

The National Agricultural Library (NAL), Document Delivery Services Branch accepts ILL requests from libraries via several electronic services. All requests must comply with established routing and referral policies and procedures. The transmitting library will pay all fees incurred during the creation of requests and communication with NAL. A sample format for ILL requests is printed below along with a list of the required data/format elements.

ELECTRONIC MAIL - **(Sample form below)**

SYSTEM	ADDRESS CODE

INTERNET .... LENDING@NALUSDA.GOV
ONTYME................................. NAL/LB
TWX/TELEX........................... Number is 710-828-0506 NAL LEND. This number may only be used for
                                    ILL requests.
FTS2000................................... A12NALLEND
OCLC .... NAL's symbol AGL need only be entered once, but it must be the last entry.

SAMPLE ELECTRONIC MAIL REQUEST

AG University/NAL   ILLRQ 231   4/1/93   NEED BY: 6/1/93

Interlibrary Loan Department
Agriculture University
Heartland, IA 56789

Dr. Smith Faculty Ag School

Canadian Journal of Soil Science 1988 v 68(1): 17-27
DeJong, R. Comparison of two soil-water models under semi-arid growing
conditions
Ver: AGRICOLA
Remarks: Not available at IU or in region.
NAL CA: 56.8 C162

Auth: C. Johnson   CCL   Maxcost: $15.00

MORE

TELEFACSIMILE - Telephone number is 301-504-5675. NAL accepts ILL requests via telefacsimile. Requests should be created on standard ILL forms and then faxed to NAL. NAL does not fill requests via Fax at this time.

REQUIRED DATA ELEMENTS/FORMAT

1. Borrower's address must be in block format with at least two blank lines above and below so form may be used in window envelopes.
2. Provide complete citation including verification, etc.
3. Provide authorizing official's name (request will be rejected if not included).
4. Include statement of copyright compliance if applicable.
5. Indicate willingness to pay applicable charges.
6. Include NAL call number if available.

The Status and Potential of Aquaculture in the United States: An Overview and Bibliography

Deborah T. Hanfman
National Agricultural Library
Aquaculture Information Center

National Agricultural Library
Beltsville, Maryland 20705-2351

July 1993

National Agricultural Library Cataloging Record:

Hanfman, Deborah T.
    The status and potential of aquaculture in the United States : an overview and bibliography.
    1. Aquaculture--United States--Bibliography. I. Title.
aSH34

Preface

The intent of this publication is to provide interested individuals with a statistical overview of the current status and future outlook of aquaculture in the United States.

Information contained in the narrative overview of this publication was gathered, in part, from the following sources: "Aquaculture: Situation and Outlook Report," produced by the Economic Research Service, U.S. Department of Agriculture; "Aquaculture in the United States: Status, Opportunities, and Recommendations," compiled in May 1992 by the Joint Subcommittee on Aquaculture in a report to the Federal Coordinating Council on Science, Engineering, and Technology; and "Fisheries of the United States, 1991," produced by the National Marine Fisheries Service, U.S. Department of Commerce. Additional sources were consulted for accuracy of data and textual content.

Several computerized databases were searched for citations to the literature. Selected citations are listed in this bibliography. Most citations date from 1989 to 1993 and are arranged alphabetically by the author's surname.

Databases accessed for relevant citations include: 1) ASFA (Aquatic Scienes and Fisheries Abstracts) database, produced under contract to the Food and Agriculture Organization of the United Nations by Cambridge Scientific Abstracts for a consortium of United Nations agencies and cooperating member states; and 2) AGRICOLA (AGRICultural OnLine Access), an agricultural database produced by the National Agricultural Library. In addition, a limited number of selected books and articles not found in these databases were included in the bibliography.

In addition, the Joint Subcommittee on Aquaculture, a Federal Government-wide coordinating body of 23 agency representatives, has established an "Aquaculture Statistical & Economic Analysis Task Force." This task force held an organizational meeting on September 24, 1992 in Washington, DC, represented by individuals from the government and industry sectors. This group will play a future key role in the coordination of existing statistical "collecting and reporting programs" in aquaculture.

FOR INFORMATION REGARDING LENDING SERVICES, please consult the information sheet in this publication entitled, "Document Delivery Services to Individuals."

Acknowledgments

Special appreciation is expressed to David Harvey of the Economic Research Service, U.S. Department of Agriculture, and Jim Meehan of the National Marine Fisheries Service, U.S. Department of Commerce, for peer reviewing the accompanying text for accuracy of data prior to its printing.

Dr. Henry Parker, Director, Office of Aquaculture, Cooperative State Research Service, U.S. Department of Agriculture is acknowledged for the use of information supplied in the JSA report to the Federal Coordinating Council on Science, Engineering, and Technology.

Deborah T. Hanfman
Coordinator
Aquaculture Information Center
National Agricultural Library
Room 304
Beltsville, Maryland 20705-2351

July 1993

Lightning Source UK Ltd.
Milton Keynes UK
UKHW021029051118
331792UK00020B/176/P